In the Shrill of the Night
How Roommates Respond to Crisis

The following multiple-choice questionnaire was devised to help you assess your ability to cope with a number of potential crisis situations. . . .

- It's 3:00 A.M. Your roommate has roused you from a sound sleep. She is standing over your bed, tears streaming down her cheeks, holding a meat cleaver. You ask:
  a). Am I having a nightmare?
  b). Are you and Roger fighting?
  c). Have you finally decided to enroll at the culinary institute?
  d). Is there someone in the apartment?
  e). Have I upset you in any way?

- Your roommate comes home in tattered clothing, wearing one shoe, escorted by two police officers. You ask:
  a). Rough day at work?
  b). Rusty's leash break again?
  c). You didn't shoot Roger, did you?
  d). Were you mugged?

- You come home to find your roommate agitated to the point of speechlessness and pointing to the empty TV table. You ask:
  a). Nothing good on tonight?
  b). Think the table needs refinishing?
  c). Have we been robbed?
  d). Have I upset you in any way?

What Color Is Your Toothbrush?
— Or —
The Joys Of Roommate Living

**Kate Kelly, Richard Davis
and Jeff Stone**

PUBLISHED BY POCKET BOOKS NEW YORK

Another *Original* publication of Pocket Books

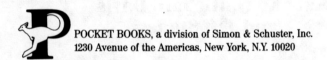

POCKET BOOKS, a division of Simon & Schuster, Inc.
1230 Avenue of the Americas, New York, N.Y. 10020

ISBN: 0-671-54337-7

First Pocket Books printing September, 1985

10 9 8 7 6 5 4 3 2 1

POCKET and colophon are registered trademarks
of Simon & Schuster, Inc.

Printed in the U.S.A.

Design by Stanley S. Drate/Folio Graphics Co., Inc.

Original drawings by Philip A. Scheuer

ACKNOWLEDGMENTS

We are grateful to the following people, who assisted in the preparation of this book in many ways. Their friendship, support, professional skills, and roommate stories are deeply appreciated:

Alpha Zingo Pow (University of Illinois chapter), Cindy Berger, Raymond Bongiovanni, Wendy Brown, Ken Diamond, William Grose, Evan Lambert, Carol Livingston, Elaine Markson, Leighton Miller, Sydny Weinberg Miner, Sally Peters, Walker Richardson, Teresa Schafer, Philip A. Scheuer, Geri Thoma, David Wachs.

We are especially indebted to the following friends who served as photo models, in addition to helping in other ways:

Eileen Albert, Alpha Epsilon Phi (Ohio State University chapter), Ty Danco, James Ellroy, Jim Fairbrother, Gerry Helferich, Sarah McKenzie Hoskins, Buffie Hughes, Bunny Kelly, Jack Kelly, Maureen Kelly, Mike Kelly, Bill Kelly, K. C. Kelly, Les Lyden, Judy O'Brien, Peter Pehrson, Lori Silverstein, Steven Witt, Duke/Duchess, Rover.

Finally, we would like to thank our families and our many, many past and present roommates, without whom this book would not have been possible or necessary.

CONTENTS

DECLARATION OF INTERDEPENDENCE

"Hell is other people."
—*Jean-Paul Sartre*

"That's life."
—*Dean Martin*

Some people think that being a roommate is a temporary thing, a phase that a young person goes through on the way to becoming an independent adult. They have the idea that after school, college, and maybe a fledgling career period, roommate days are over. They are wrong. Roommatehood is an essential condition of every stage of life, proof positive of the theory of interdependence. You will never live alone.

What Color Is Your Toothbrush?

— Or —

The Joys Of Roommate Living

1

BASIC TRAINING FOR ROOMMATES: At Home and at School

FAMILY AFFAIR:
Rooming with Parents, Siblings, Pets and Other Intimates

Someone famous once said that we begin and end life on our own. But surely this is true only in a limited, technical sense. From the moment of conception, we share a warm, comfortable space with Mother—the most accommodating roommate we will ever know. After emerging from this prenatal arrangement, most of us bunk with brothers and sisters. We learn early on that the only really satisfying ways of handling conflict with a roommate are:

1). Destroy his favorite possessions.
2). Kill him.

Rooming in the Womb

Although none of us is likely to remember the warm, intimate accommodations of the first nine months of life, scientists have provided extensive documentation and illustration of the primal home.

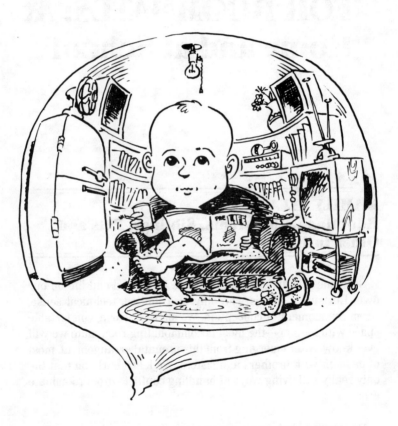

Clearly, the womb is the prototypical rooming arrangement. Food, for instance, is a potential issue in all roommate situations. The unborn child cannot verbally express dietary preferences. However, compliments or complaints can be sent through a variety of behavior, such as kicking, punching, stroking and waking Mother up in the middle of the night. These techniques may also be employed in desperation by older roommates when verbal discourse fails.

Similarly, it is in the womb that a baby is first exposed to a roommate's potentially repugnant personal habits, such as smoking, drinking and taking drugs. Sexual habits can also cause conflicts. Baby may feel that Mother does not consider his schedule and privacy in planning her love life.

The experience of sharing womb space with a sibling offers an even better introduction to the roommate problems likely to develop in later life. Opposite schedules, deciding who sleeps where, assertion of territorial rights and many other issues will certainly arise.

Finally, the fetal child is subjected to one of the most troubling of rooming situations—eviction. Each baby is bound to an approximately nine-month lease. Renewal, however, is impossible, and there is no legal recourse.

SIBLING RIVALRY:
Hand-to-Hand Combat

As a child and a roommate, you must learn to defend yourself. You have met the enemy and he is your brother and/or sister.

For the most part, keeping a wary eye cocked toward the imaginary Demilitarized Zone (DMZ) in your bedroom will be defense enough. But you must always be ready for an incursion. Knowing the signs of an impending attack in your room or at the dinner table will enable you to protect yourself and may even shift the balance of power in your favor:

1). When doing your homework in your room, beware of your sibling roommate's seemingly innocent behavior. He or she may just be lulling you into a false sense of security so as to snatch your carefully penned arithmetic lesson or essay on your summer vacation.

2). Keep weapons handy to repel attacks of this nature. Your pillow is especially good for temporarily stunning your attacker, while you hunt for a new weapon or call in one of the superpowers downstairs by shouting, "Mom! Dad!"

3). Be especially watchful for lightning raids at the dinner table. Generally, table attacks will be less grievous than those in the bedroom, but still warlike in intent.

4). Carefully establish an imaginary DMZ between you and your sibling, and make sure the superpowers at the table know where the DMZ is located in case of incursion.

5). Watch for sudden movements of your sibling's hand: It may be wielding a carefully loaded forkful of mashed potatoes or another instrument of dining room warfare.

6). If both superpowers should become engaged in détente between themselves, use their inattention to local affairs as an opportunity to strike before your sibling has the chance. Shove his or her peas into the mashed potatoes where, even when ordered to "clean the plate" by the superpowers, he or she certainly won't eat them. Your sibling's dessert is doubtless going to be a casualty of the attack.

7). Be sure to retreat from the DMZ before the superpowers have noticed your offensive. Otherwise, the balance of power will shift against you, resulting in loss of face and, perhaps, banishment from the dinner table.

8). Ultimate weapons: full glass of milk, gravy pitcher. Don't forget to say "I'm sorry," or someone will think you did it on purpose.

He ain't heavy, He's my brother

Sibling rivalry aside, rooming with an older brother is not a totally unpleasant experience. You have companionship, a role model and someone to pester when that pesty feeling comes upon you. Rooming with a younger brother, however, is always an unpleasant experience.

Brothers will always be consigned together to a room that has a bunk bed. As they get older, the bunk bed will be dismantled and twin beds will replace it. The logistics of who sleeps in the top bunk in early brother rooming and how far apart the beds will be in later brother rooming are crucial to the peace and stability of the family at large.

In brother rooming the basics always remain the same:

Bunks will have identical sheets and bedspreads.
Wallpaper will be Revolutionary War or Wild West motif.
Older brother will have intricately assembled models.
Younger brother will break them. Or be accused of breaking them.
Christmas gifts will be identical, except for size and color.
Brothers will be forced to sit in the back seat together on long trips.
If one brother throws up/yawns/laughs, the other will throw up/yawn/laugh a few minutes later.
Older brother will never want younger brother to play on his team. Mom or Dad will make older brother let younger brother play.
Unless one brother is mortally wounded, they will always answer "Nothing" when parents holler, "What's going on up there?"
Older brother is the first to get his own room or leave home. Younger brother is first overjoyed, then envious, then lonely.
Brothers will go to the same school until college, when they will choose universities at opposite ends of the country.

TWISTED SISTERS

Sisters who room together tend to the extreme. When they're getting along, they're the best of friends. When they're not getting along, they're feuding like the Hatfields and the McCoys.

When getting along:

1). They tell each other their innermost, deepest, darkest, cross-your-heart-and-hope-to-die secrets.

2). They will let their sister wear anything they own, including gold chains and angora sweaters.

3). They giggle together for hours, for reasons no other living being can fathom.

4). They will share all makeup.

When not getting along:

They blurt out these secrets at the dinner table or on the extension phone when their sister is talking to a cute boy.

They ransack their sister's dresser drawers in search of real and imagined borrowed items.

They can maintain a mutual vow of silence longer than the most pious nun.

They will say, "Keep your herpes off my lipstick."

THE PAJAMA GAME

The childhood and adolescent years provide numerous opportunities for spending the night outside the family home, all of which serve as excellent preparation for adult rooming.

The Slumber Party

The essential requirements:

1). The slumber party room must be located as far away as possible from the host parents' bedroom.

2). Pull-out sofa beds and blanket tents in the living room are acceptable. Basement, screened porch or outdoor tent accommodations receive highest ratings, however.

3). Specially created snacks, such as pigs-in-blankets, mini-pizzas and marshmallow–Rice Krispies squares. Snack food is first offered by host parents, later pilfered from kitchen behind their backs.

4). Participants must be willing to stay awake all night long.

5). The tolerance of the host parents must be tested to the limit.

6). Games must be played.

INDOOR GAMES

Indoor games generally require a "patsy"—the least popular of the children at the party. The patsy is further designated by:

1). An inability to stay awake all night.
2). A desire to respect the host parents' household.

Once the patsy is positively identified, the fun can begin. Favorite rituals include:

1). Freezing the patsy's underwear.
2). Putting the hand of the sleeping patsy into a pan of tepid water.
3). Squeezing toothpaste onto the patsy's face.
4). Short-sheeting the patsy's sleeping bag. (Only a patsy brings a sheet for his/her sleeping bag.)

Some indoor games are played only with visitors from slumber parties of the opposite sex:

1). Post Office
2). Spin the Bottle
3). Doctor
4). Strip Poker

3

OUTDOOR GAMES

Outdoor games call for the slumber party group to sneak out of the house in the middle of the night. (Since the patsy would spoil the fun, he or she must be asleep, sedated or gagged.) The revelers then proceed to:

1). Chalk sidewalks (especially popular among girls, who commit such messages to the pavement as "Linda Loves Davie 4-ever," frequently in a heart-shaped motif).

2). Soap car windows.

3). Decorate bushes and small trees with toilet paper.

4). Ignite firecrackers and other small explosives in neighborhood mailboxes.

5). Turn on garden hoses and sprinklers.

6). Tip over birdbaths, gazing globes and other garden ornaments.

7). Visit other slumber parties.

Special note for apartment dwellers:

Many outdoor games must be adapted to suit the urban environment. Some especially popular variations are:

1). Ringing all the doorbells in the hallway.

2). Riding the elevator and stopping at every floor.

3). Mixing up all the doormats in the hallway.

4). Dumping liquid detergent in all the dryers in the laundry room.

The Advanced Slumber Party

Slumber parties for older adolescents have special character-istics:

1). They usually include members of both sexes.

2). They depend on host parents being absent (preferably on a three-week Mediterranean cruise).

3). They feature experimentation with sex and controlled substances.

4). The ideal chaperone is an older sibling of legal drinking age, with driver's license.

5). The advanced slumber party is not confined to a single room, but spreads, like wildfire, through the entire house.

ACTIVITIES

No organized games are scheduled. Nevertheless, entertainments such as the following are noteworthy:

1). Filling out subscription coupons for porno magazines and the *Frederick's of Hollywood* catalog in the name of the junior high principal

2). Composing blackmail letters to the mayor (mailing of letters is optional)

3). Conducting a raiding party into the chaperone sibling's bedroom, preferably when sibling is also entertaining an overnight guest

4). Reading dirty magazines. (If *Playboy* and *Penthouse* are not available, old issues of *National Geographic* or *Gynecology World* will do.)

Summer Camp

Though the camp environment is more structured than the standard slumber party, the main object—having fun by breaking as many rules as possible—remains the same.

At camp, the patsy must be bribed or beaten into serving as decoy. The patsy is instructed to cry out, at 3:00 A.M., such lines as:

1). "I need a drink of water."
2). "I have to go to the bathroom."
3). "I want to go to the nurse's cabin."

This will generally eliminate the counselor for sufficient time to:

1). Sabotage the counselor's bed and/or personal effects
2). Sneak out of the cabin for:
    a). midnight swims.
    b). hide-and-seek games in the woods.
    c). raids on the dining hall.
    d). raids on cabins containing members of the opposite sex.

TEENAGE SEX AT HOME:
(I Can't Get No) Satisfaction

It may seem odd that you develop a healthy interest in the opposite sex long before you have the privacy to pursue your healthy interest properly. You may still room with your brother or sister. If you have a room of your own, it is in your parents' house. Generally, your parents want you to postpone this particular healthy interest for a few years.

These circumstances force you to exercise extreme ingenuity. There are several locales where you can grope and fumble about while avoiding parents and sibling roommates, though each has its own risks.

IN YOUR ROOM

Some teenagers spurn the car for lack of license or because the family Chevette isn't suitable for dating. Carefully calculating when no one will be home, they attempt to lure romance to the house at the appropriate times. This requires the strategic planning capabilities of the Joint Chiefs of Staff, plus the raw nerve of Acapulco cliff divers. People who try to use their rooms for a romantic tryst are inevitably caught and suffer irreversible psychological damage.

YOUR BEST FRIEND'S HOUSE

This is difficult to arrange and is considered tacky under the best of circumstances. Usually, the strangeness of the situation puts everyone off, and you end up going to the Dairy Queen instead.

THE CAR PARKED IN THE GARAGE

Sometimes, gearshifts are positioned more effectively than chaperones. Sexual experimentation in such an environment may lead to serious injury, whether the car is in operation or not. Also, you'll be discovered when Mom goes to aerobics.

YOUR PARENTS' ROOM

Never!

ROOMING AS GROOMING FOR SUCCESS: The College Years

There are many conventional measures of collegiate success, only one of which is the cumulative grade point average. But the most telling indicator of *future* success is the student's ability to share living space.

Measuring students' competence as roommates is difficult—there are no standardized tests, though students with siblings or previous boarding school experience have an edge.

Congenial rooming, like success later in life, is possible only when one understands the skills involved and applies them to the situation at hand. Or at least appears to.

FRESHMAN YEAR

Creating the optimum roommate environment is a particular challenge for freshmen dorm dwellers. Though eager for the "independent and flexible" (read "orgiastic") lifestyle offered by today's colleges, freshmen generally have had no experience living as adults away from home. To prevent the young adults from making major errors in choosing roommates, the college kindly takes this otherwise adult task out of their hands.

The Dean's Decision
Pomp and Circumstance

Reputedly benevolent deans of housing committees screen freshman dorm candidates and create what they feel will be ideal personality combinations.

"This stalwart football player/accounting major from Alabama and that introspective poet/molecular biophysics major from Boston will have much to share with each other," they muse. "And since it's a coed dorm, let's put them next to that lovely Vietnamese girl who doesn't speak English yet and her roommate, the prep school field hockey star whose father endowed the new sports center. They'll be a great bridge foursome."

The outcome: The poet and the Vietnamese girl will lock eyes upon first meeting, form a searing spiritual bond, and move off campus together as soon as possible. They will never emerge from their apartment for the next four years except to go to the library (together) and for exams.

The jock and jockette, attracted by mutual athletic prowess, have a brief fling. Then the call of the gridiron and brew with the boys seduces the football hero away from his preppie amour. Besides, she was a threat to his masculinity anyway. She feels intensely relieved at the neat demise of their relationship—after all, how could she bring that unrefined lout home to Mummy and Daddy?

Moving In

Moving into the college dorm is an exciting and altogether telling event. It is important for everyone involved to make a first impression that is both honest and positive. Unfortunately, these two qualities do not often travel together.

The student should think twice about expressing personal hopes, habits and hobbies. What seems normal to one person often seems quite peculiar (or offensive) to others.

You may like to keep a log of your sexual conquests. Nevertheless, displaying this log in poster form on your bedroom door may encourage your roommate to add unsolicited and embarrassing comments.

Your family entourage should be restrained as well. You may permit your eleven-year-old brother Rusty to wrestle with the family Great Dane, Rastro, on your bed at home. But your new roommate may not want them treating hers like center ring at Madison Square Garden.

Further advice:

1). Deny your mother the opportunity to spend the first night in the dorm room with you.

2). The same goes for your high school girl friend or boyfriend, even if she or he is attending the same college.

3). Refrain from practicing your trombone in the room.

4). Do not commence the study of a new musical instrument in the room. *Ever.*

5). Confine the placement of religious shrines to unshared locations such as desk drawers and closets.

6). Restrict early morning exercise (especially karate or yoga rituals that require loud screaming or mantras) to closets, deserted bathrooms, and isolated exercise rooms in the university gym.

7). Avoid placing your dart board in the vicinity of your roommate's antique crystal collection or signed Picasso pen-and-inks.

8). Veil your true beliefs in the prophecies of Ouija until the board tells you otherwise.

9). Never bring lab work in nuclear fission back to the dorm room.

10). Save discussions of sexual habits and preferences for later—unless you will be exercising them within the next few hours.

CLIQUES THAT DON'T CLICK

Although they may share a room, certain students will avoid each other like the plague. Imagine these volatile combinations of roomies:

THE FEMINIST AND THE FRAT GROUPIE

The feminist holds consciousness-raising sessions and candlelight vigils at scenes of sexual exploitation. The frat groupie is furious when the feminist takes legal action to close down the "animal house." The frat guys think the feminist is probably a lesbian, anyway. But if she'd just dress up, put on some makeup and lose weight, the frat groupie would consider taking her to a toga party.

THE RICH FOREIGN STUDENT AND THE POOR FOREIGN STUDENT

The rich foreign student leads a glamorous, jet-set existence: posh parties, designer clothes, and a clubby relationship with rich Americans. Back home, the rich foreigner employs people like the poor foreigner as house servants. The rich foreigner wants a squash partner, somebody who knows a lot of girls or a good dope connection in a roommate.

Unfortunately, the poor foreign student is too busy reading Karl Marx and slinging hash in the dining hall to fill the bill.

THE SOCIALITE AND THE NERD

The socialite is the life of the party. The nerd is not, and does not understand that the virtues of her new quad disk drive are not a universally fascinating subject of conversation. The nerd sighs longingly as the socialite heads off to the right parties. The nerd will make "Some Mores," pick zits and watch reruns of "The Love Boat" in the dorm.

THE ARTISTE AND THE MBA

From an early age, the life of the artiste has been one long struggle against Philistines, and he hates to have to associate with them in college. Of course, the artiste's love affair with painting, dance, video or South Indian droning has been lavishly subsidized by doting bourgeois parents. The MBA is disturbed by the artiste's lack of responsibility, questionable sexuality, and repugnant personal habits.

HOW TO LIVE WITH A BMOC (Big Man On Campus) or BWOC (Big Woman on Campus)

Living with a BMOC or BWOC is not easy, but it does have its rewards. Sometimes a person carries that special status from the very beginning of his or her college career. Or the distinction may occur suddenly. A person may be elected to an office, perform heroics on the athletic field or establish a major drug connection.

The key to living with a campus luminary is humility. To be even tolerably happy, you must know your place and accept it: You will henceforth be known primarily as the BMOC's or BWOC's roommate.

But being Number 2 isn't all bad. You are like the First Lady, the Vice President or the Queen Consort. You are secure in your place of honor, but you are not in the top spot. So here's the deal. You get reflected glory and a lot of perks. In exchange, you have to do just two things:

1). Agree with everything your roommate says.

2). Keep any potentially embarrassing secrets to yourself—like the BMOC's teddy bear Sam, which sits patiently on his pillow waiting for him to come to bed; or the silver-studded black leather outfit the BWOC likes to lounge around in.

WHY JOHNNY CAN'T STUDY

Some students require all the comforts of home in order to settle down and get to work:

1). The cozy chair.
2). The continually replenished coffee mug.
3). The favorite records on the stereo.

Others prefer the more austere environment of a library or study room.

The more outdoorsy or artistic student may wish to commune with nature while studying. He or she will therefore choose the busiest area of the campus in which to sit cross-legged on the grass.

Conflicts may arise, however, if both roommates like to study in the room.

Problem 1: One likes to listen to Van Halen, while the other prefers the sounds of silence.
Solution 1: Headphones.

Problem 2: One loves to eat potato chips or celery while gnawing away at Renaissance history. The other longs for that roommate's teeth to fall out.
Solution 2: See Solution 1.

If you simply can't stand working in the room together, try staggering your study hours. If this proves unsuccessful, try:
Solution 3: Do your own homework and your roommate's one night; have your roommate do it all the next night, and so forth.

The real problems crop up when one roommate likes to study in the room and the other prefers to *party* there.

The studious roommate may complain that he or she can't work well anywhere but in the room. The social animal will reply that it is totally impossible for him or her to entertain in the library.

If you are the hard-working victim of such a situation, try one of the following techniques and just see if you aren't back at your favorite study spot soon:

1). Attend one of your roommate's parties. Remark pleasantly how unfortunate it is that no one on the "A" list could come.

2). Borrow a quarantine sign from the infirmary, slap it on the door to your room, and let word out that you have been stricken with mononucleosis/hepatitis/cholera/diphtheria/typhoid, or any combination of the above.

3). Sit down at your desk and try to study while the hubbub goes on around you. You won't get anything done, and you may have to repeat this tactic once or twice. But sooner or later your roommate will decide that you are either a nut case or very sincere about wanting to study in the room.

Ex loco parentis:
Off-Campus Living

There are certain individualists who eschew living with those men or women whose identity rests in playing intramural sports, and whose knowledge of the Greek alphabet is confined to the letters above their fraternity/sorority doors. These free spirits often opt for a less structured living situation known as off-campus housing.

Indeed, they frequently band together in imitation of fraternity/sorority houses, but without the highly developed Greek hierarchy. Besides, crawling around on all fours to gain admittance to a living situation should be saved for cities where finding an apartment is *really* tough.

For lack of a better word, let's call these off-campus houses sofrorities.

A sofrority is a decrepit old Victorian house just off campus.

It must have five to ten housemates in the same curriculum.

It has almost no furniture, and must have the most sophisticated stereo equipment currently available. The system is wired so that music is played through professional quality speakers in every room of the house. The volume must be kept very high at all times. (The Grateful Dead requested the loan of this sound system when they played on campus last year.)

There is a great deal of studying going on in this house at all times, but members never study at the same time.

One housemate must be seriously into drugs.

At least three girlfriends or boyfriends will have changed hands by the end of the semester.

A party must be held on every night of the weekend—that is, Wednesday, Thursday, Friday, Saturday and Sunday.

Dormitory types will flock to these parties.

At least half the stereo equipment will disappear by the end of the semester.

At least one housemate will do incredibly well and go on to a top grad school.

At least one housemate will have an expensive sports car.

The car will be totaled by another member of the house before the end of the semester.

At least one housemate will have an excellent relationship with the little old man or little old lady who owns the house. This housemate is adept at explaining away the car in the backyard, the attrition of the windows, and the noise complaints.

At least one housemate will be indicted by a grand jury before the end of the semester.

At least one of the housemates will renege on the rent/phone/electric bill(s).

At least two of the housemates will be the nucleus for another off-campus house the next semester.

Knocking on Heaven's Door— Collegiate Sex

The logistics of collegiate sex can be mind-boggling—especially if you happen to share sleeping quarters with a roommate.

Most roommates are considerate enough to warn others not to enter the room while they are scaling the heights of ecstasy. These signals include:

1). Looping a knotted tie around the door handle.

2). Screaming, "Don't come in!"

3). Leaving a note pinned to the door saying, "I'm entertaining."

If your roommate is already in bed (alone) and you are returning to the room with a proverbial hot number, you are faced with a different type of dilemma. Courses of action include:

1). Suggest to the hot number that you go to his or her place for the night.

2). Assure your companion that, "My roommate sleeps like a log." Or: "He/she can't possibly wake up." Then proceed to your room as planned.

3). Check into a hotel.

Just remember that the burden of embarrassment always falls on the wakers rather than on the wakees.

Even when roommates sleep in separate rooms, dormitory and apartment walls are often so thin that they leave few details to the imagination. Room layouts, too, are frequently far from ideal. Watching a string of your roommate's mates saunter through your room night after night is not exactly like watching the Macy's Thanksgiving Day Parade. It can be trying even to the most voyeuristic of souls.

There is one advantage in witnessing the string of your roommate's lovers, however: You can make damned sure your own honey doesn't get added to it.

Of course, the only thing worse than knowing other people are having fun in bed is not having fun in bed yourself. It helps to have another unattached roommate at a time like this. You can remind each other that it's the other people, not you, who should be embarrassed. And at least you're not the only one alone under the sheets.

BATHROOMS

Bathrooms may be as much a source of sexual embarrassment as bedrooms.

Contraceptive paraphernalia left out in plain sight, for instance, can create difficult moments with a host of people:

1). Your virgin roommate who asks where you bought that odorless, scentless toothpaste.

2). Your visiting parents.

3). Your little sister. "No, those are not vitamins in a convenient dispenser."

The considerate roommate will store sensitive items discreetly.

GOING STEADY

If you and your roommate both have steady boyfriends or girlfriends, you will want to work out a system so that both couples are not occupying the same room at the same time.

Solution 1: Plan to alternate nights and weekends away from the room.

Though this solution is generally satisfactory, the situation becomes more complicated when the boyfriends or girlfriends also have roommates with whom they must coordinate their plans.

Solution 2: Have a meeting of all the intimates involved and set up a calendar of who sleeps where and when.

Though a more rash and, perhaps, impersonal solution, this is practical. Anyway, all roommates aren't usually having affairs at the same time. If they were, a tremendous room displacement effect would set in all across campus.

And no one would know where not to say someone else was when their parents called.

3

FOR WHOM THE BELL TOLLS: Non-Romantic Cohabitation

After the long years of education comes the high point and the low point of the roommate experience. You get a place with other people like yourself, with whom you can share the fun and frustration of being young, single and working.

Now there are no parents or deans to whom you can complain, "She won't stop borrowing my jewelry," or, "He is a sociopathic weirdo."

Congratulations.

You're finally on your own in the wonderful world of rooming.

YOU'RE THE ONE I WANT: Finding a Roommate

Finally, you have graduated from college and found a great job. You have to move to a city where you have a few acquaintances, but they all have established living situations. You know you will have to share to get by on the starting salary. What are your options?

1). Convince a college friend to change plans and relocate with you.

Remember that in this case you will bear heavy responsibility for the future of your new roommate. You will have to support *her* if she was planning to go to Harvard Law and you convinced her you needed her in Fort Worth. You will have to answer to *him* when he finds out that there are not many opportunities for a nuclear physicist in Iron Tongue, Minnesota.

2). Talk to your new employer about the possibility of rooming with someone already at that company.

The drawback here is that as a college graduate you are supposed to be able to handle living in the real world. Begging your new employer for help before you make him even a single penny will put you in a bad light, and you will probably spend the next twenty years returning the favor.

3). Read ads in the local paper for apartment shares.

This form of roommate roulette is extremely tricky and you must be prepared for the worst. It will happen.

Let's Get Personal: The Want Ads

There are basically three types of publications in which you will find these "share" ads: the regular city newspaper, the local counterculture paper, and the special interest or trade magazine of your profession. (*Note:* We have not mentioned other special interest magazines, which feature nifty leather restraining devices or use the word "swingle.")

The regular city newspaper will not necessarily have the most desirable listings, despite the relative respectability of those listed. Many more established folks, those between the ages of eighty and one hundred five, list with the major newspaper.

By the same token, the counterculture paper will not necessarily have the most "loonies." Young professionals and college students like to feel that they have been perpetually "tuned in" and are naturally hip, even if they wear a three-piece suit every day and manage stocks and bonds.

Your trade publication will have two listings, both of which have been in the magazine for the last three years running.

HOW TO READ THE ADS

WHAT THE AD SAYS:

> Prof. M, has big 1 bdr to share.
> Nice neighborhood, good trans.
> $325 mo. not incl. util.
> M or F OK. By May 1.

WHAT THE AD MEANS:

This is either a professor or a professional male. (God knows what a professional male would be like to live with.) He has a tiny cramped apartment with a bedroom the size of a foreign car's glove compartment.

You are going to be sleeping in the living room. Most likely on the floor.

You will have to arm yourself and dress in camouflage to get from the apartment to the bus or train, which will take you to within a mile or so of the two other buses or trains you will need to connect with to get to a place where you can rent a car to get to work.

Your share of the rent (be aware this may be the entire actual rent) is $325 dollars American, in cash, no checks please, to be paid 15 days in advance of the rent due date, notwithstanding the $650 deposit, non-returnable if you leave without giving 24 months' notice.

Utilities, including the cold-water bill, come to around $325 a month.

Male or Female OK means he is a lonely guy—but at least not a lonely guy looking for another lonely guy. He would much rather have a female move in, but he is too smart to say *Female only.* Then everyone who calls will think he is a girl looking for a girl-only situation.

By May 1. He is being evicted on May 1.

Another drawback to the ads—other than that they are misleading, are placed by deviants of every stripe, and are extremely time-consuming and depressing—is that they don't differentiate between those who decorate their apartments with orange crates and those who prefer storing everything in Hefty bags.

WOULD YOU BUY A USED CAR FROM THIS MAN?: The Agency Route

Many large cities have agencies that screen potential apartment-mates to save you the trouble and trauma of the want ads.

If you are looking to move into someone else's apartment, you simply go to the agency and pay a fee—usually not more than an amount equal to six months' worth of your salary—and fill out a questionnaire of surprising length and detail.

Then they give you a list of apartments—the same list they were going to give you before you filled out the questionnaire—and inform you that you can call in for more listings the next day, when they will give you the same list of apartments they gave you the day before. Off you go to meet every weirdo, child rapist, dope fiend and lonely middle-aged lady the city has to offer.

If you have an apartment to share, you read agency ads like the following:

BOOMER ROOMERS

We are the most exclusive roommate referral service in the city. We have 50 years' experience in matching the right people to suitable rooming situations. We carefully screen all applicants and match you with a person of similar tastes and background. There is no fee for this service to those listing their apartments with us.

Suitably impressed, you call them up for your interview.

The irritated voice on the other end of the line then puts you on hold for ten or fifteen minutes before saying:

"So what kinda apartment you got? How much? When ya want somebody in dere?" Whereupon they send you a healthy sampling of all the transient, incompetent, irresponsible degenerates who have ever passed through your city.

I KNOW A GUY WHO KNOWS A GUY

The easiest, safest and most sensible way to find a roommate has always been through people you know and like.

Even this course can be dangerous. It may jeopardize you and your roommate's friendship with your common friend, if things don't work out. The cardinal rule is that roommates, unlike diamonds, are not forever. You must always be aware of the future implications of your living situation.

THE WOMEN

THE SUPER PROFESSIONAL

She works as an account executive for an advertising firm. Spends most of her time at the agency. Dresses impeccably. Is always polite to the neighbors in the hallway. Married to her career, she doesn't have time for a husband right now. She lets you use her maid for free and works from 5:00 A.M. to 10:00 P.M. when she is in town. The only drawback is that she will give you the most monumental inferiority complex you have had since your older sister starting going out with the guy you had a big crush on in high school.

THE ARTIST

She dresses in the funkiest clothes available from Goodwill. May not speak to you for days. Goes to Europe every year. Never dates—men, anyway. Works part-time for a gallery or experimental theater. She is likely to be very sloppy, but will expect the highest degree of consideration from you, especially when she is "creating" whatever it is she creates. She will attempt to get you to discuss things you have no interest in with witty opening lines like, "Do you think Pollack was attempting to re-define a new modernist perspective?"

THE PARTY GIRL

She works as a secretary for a respectable company. Can't have a career since only a straight 9-to-5 job with at least a two-hour lunch will fit into her social schedule. Always has a dozen friends over at all hours. Manages twenty dates and two or three blow-out parties a month. She will borrow your albums and never put the records back in the sleeves. Always wants to dance. Can you stand this much fun?

THE HOMEBODY

She works at home. Has a small business making teddy bears or doing free-lance pottery design. Feeds your pets when you are away. If you don't mind the fact that she hasn't left the apartment in the last two years, and the kiln in the living room doesn't offend your sense of proper décor, she is a very good roommate to have. Buy some pottery.

THE SOCIALITE

She is the most beautiful woman you have ever seen, and dressed to the nines. Hardly ever home, she gets picked up in limos a lot. You haven't the foggiest as to why she is looking for a roommate. Always smiles. Great teeth. Forget it—wherever she lives, you can't afford it.

THE GUYS

THE CONFIRMED BACHELOR

He can afford to live alone, but he can take an extra two weeks in Vail at his new condo if you pay half the rent. Often visited by overnight guests whom you never see again, he seems to own an inexhaustible supply of toothbrushes. Occasionally, you will be roused as he creeps in at 5:00 A.M., impeccably dressed in his Brooks Brothers suit, to pick up his briefcase on the way to the office. He is good for subscriptions to *Time* and *Ad Age* at least, and you might even borrow his *Playboys* (he loves the articles). He likes to have women as roommates, since this gives his apartment that "feminine" touch. Also, he likes to have a female roommate around to provide company (the nonromantic kind) when he is between girlfriends.

THE PSYCHOPATH

If this freak didn't need you to come up with rent (he says you're paying half, but it's actually the whole thing), you wouldn't be there at all. He never seems to go to bed. He likes to order out for food since the bright light of day apparently hurts his eyes. You often hear strange sounds coming from his room. He stares at you a lot. Never invite him to parties, since he will sit in the corner and make everybody nervous. Has a boa constrictor named Nietzsche. If you find yourself living with him, pack.

THE NICE GUY

He's fairly good-looking. Has a respectable job but lacks ambition. Wants to move to the suburbs as soon as he can afford to get married. Very concerned about the building. Kills giant bugs for lady neighbors. Knows how to listen, great to take to parties. You were thinking about setting him up with your friend Jane, until you noticed he is even nice to the psychopath who lives across the hall.

THE GAY MAN

Depending on your own sexual orientation, he can be a very good or a very bad roommate. However, if you need someone to confide your deepest secrets to, agree that all the good ones are either married or gay, like to have an apartment Halston would die for, and appreciate the latest trends in cuisine, he might be right for you.

THE WILD AND CRAZY GUY

If you would like to pretend you are back in college, this is your guy. Always cracking jokes and cheering you up, he has an endless stream of friends in and out of the apartment. Generally makes a serious pass at three to four women per party. Frequently disappears for days or even weeks at a time. Returns with a major hangover, dressed in a Hawaiian shirt and wearing sunglasses. Often forgets to pay the rent. No food in the refrigerator, but a bar that could service Studio 54.

SPECIAL CASES

THE OVER-THIRTY ROOMMATE

A particularly interesting breed of cat. First of all, they most likely live in an apartment, even though they think they ought to live in a house. Their families keep telling them they ought to be married, too. They feel slightly foolish about living much as they did in college, but the diminished buying power of their dollar and reduced career expectations have trapped them in a roommate situation.

THE YOUNG MARRIEDS

Very good about making the place into a home. Also, they have loads of single friends they will be more than happy to introduce you to. You will always be outnumbered in any kind of decision making, however, and if one spouse does side with you, the other will not speak to you for seven to ten days. You will never be able to ask what all those groans were last night. Even when they are having a tiff and it sounds as if they might kill each other, you will never be able to call the police. By the time the police arrive, they will be in bed, making up.

THE PROSPECTIVE ROOMMATE QUESTIONNAIRE, OR HOW TO AVOID LIVING WITH AN AX MURDERER

Roommate relationships, like marriages, often fail because the parties involved simply don't know each other well enough at the beginning. One step you can take to try to make sure your roommate relationship doesn't end in disaster is to administer the following questionnaire to any prospective cohabitors.

Of course, we can't guarantee that you won't end up with an ax murderer anyway. They're generally the nice, normal-seeming people about whom it is always said, "No one ever would have thought . . ."

SMOKER OR NON-SMOKER

1. Do you smoke?

( ) Yes   ( ) No

If yes, what and how often?_____

_____

BATHROOM USAGE

2. What hours of the day do you regularly use the bathroom?

a. ( ) 6:30 A.M.–7:00 A.M.   ( ) 7:00 A.M.–7:30 A.M.

   ( ) 7:30 A.M.–8 A.M.

b. ( ) 10:30 P.M.–11:00 P.M.   ( ) 11:00 P.M.–11:30 P.M.

   ( ) 11:30 P.M.–Midnight

*c. ( ) None of the above

*d. ( ) All of the above

3. What color is your toothbrush?_____

*Are you a dental floss grubber?_____

*Instant disqualifier

4. Your toiletries would fit into a:

( ) Briefcase   ( ) Overnight case   ( ) Steamer trunk

( ) Walk-in closet

SEXUALITY

5. **Sexual preferences, if any:**_____
   If yes, please indicate which of the following:
   ( ) Public   ( ) Private
   With whom?_____
   How often?_____
   Where?_____
   How loud? (decibels?)_____

6. **Approximately how many times a week do you entertain overnight guests?**
   ( ) Once   ( ) Twice   ( ) Three times   ( ) Four times
   ( ) Five times   ( ) All week   ( ) Never
   If yes, expected additional bathroom time?_____
   Special disinfectants required?_____

KITCHEN USAGE

7. **The most accurate description of your cooking skills is:**
   ( ) FIRESTARTER
   Canned, frozen and packaged foods almost exclusively. You can make lettuce and tomato salads from scratch, however. Utensils required include can opener, saucepan, spoon, knife, glass, bowl, microwave. (Can you survive without microwave?_____)
   ( ) SHORT ORDER
   Have mastered two or three reasonably palatable, legitimate dishes you can cook from scratch. Have attempted to create unique and savory cuisine with aid of Pierre Franey and James Beard. Bulk of culinary adventures, however, have been inspired by the feast/orgy scene from the film *Tom Jones,* and have taken place in finer restaurants everywhere.
   ( ) CORDON BLEU COOKING SCHOOL GRADUATE
   You wish to exchange consummate cooking skills for room and board, prepare sumptuous repasts for roommate(s). (Do you also do windows?_____)

PETS

8. **Are you a pet owner?**
   ( ) Yes   ( ) No
   a. Dogs

TYPE OF DOG:
( ) Teeny-tiny   ( ) Cute and yappy   ( ) Draught animal
( ) Acceptable breed
TEMPERAMENT:
( ) Lassie   ( ) Old Yeller   ( ) Cujo
SLEEPING HABITS:
( ) On floor   ( ) On bed
( ) On furniture
If yes, whose?_____
OTHER:
( ) Rug despoiler   ( ) Bone hider   ( ) Slobberer
( ) Leg humper   ( ) Crotch sniffer

b. Cats

TYPE OF CAT:
( ) Alley   ( ) Siamese   ( ) Persian   ( ) Ocelot or larger
TOILET:
( ) Litter box   ( ) Potty   ( ) Bathtub
TEMPERAMENT:
( ) Finicky   ( ) Friendly   ( ) Indifferent   ( ) Dangerous
OTHER:
( ) Declawed   ( ) Shedder   ( ) "Present" bringer
( ) Sprayer
( ) Likes to knead face of human in early morning hours
If yes, only your face or other people's, too?_____

c. Birds

TYPE:
( ) Talker (Rating—circle one: G, PG, R, X, XXX) ( ) Squawker
( ) Singer (Circle one: Rock, Jazz, Easy Listening, C&W, Classical
Heavy Metal)
OTHER:
( ) Newspaper trained   ( ) Disease potential
( ) Poultry dinner potential

d. Reptiles

TYPE:
( ) Poisonous if it bites   ( ) Lethal if it hugs
( ) Slimy   ( ) Dry   ( ) Plumbing clogger
DIET:
( ) Animal (Circle one: dead or alive)   ( ) Vegetable
Snake owners, please answer following questions:

Do you have unresolved sexual conflicts?_____

Are you planning a trip to the Amazon?_____

Have you ever thought you were Cleopatra in a previous life?_____

Do you play a flute-like musical instrument?_____

e. **Rodents**

( ) Male ( ) Female ( ) Both

( ) Caged ( ) Uncaged

If uncaged, answer the following:

Ratio of tooth size to body size?_____

OTHER:

( ) You own videocassettes of "Ben" and "Willard"

( ) You are privately seeking a cure for cancer

( ) You free-lance or do moonlight work in the "fun fur" business

( ) You will sign an iron-clad agreement to recapture—dead or alive—if rodent pet escapes from cage

f. **Fish**

ACCOMMODATION:

( ) Bowl ( ) Modest aquarium

( ) Tanks rivaling Sea World

FOOD:

( ) Animal ( ) Vegetable ( ) Flake ( ) Human

OTHER:

Frequency of reproduction?_____

Suitable for Sushi in a pinch?_____

Kept for atmosphere, company or lack of imagination?_____

_____

Have you ever fantasized about any of the following?

( ) Jacques Cousteau ( ) Flipper

( ) Captain Nemo ( ) Lloyd Bridges

g. **Other pets**

( ) You have always felt a need to be different

If yes, how different are you?_____

How will this affect potential roommate situations?_____

_____

Will you expect me to be different, too?_____

CLEANING

9. Cleaning is:

( ) Something you don't believe in.

( ) Something you believe in only in theory.

( ) A torture technique invented by nagging mothers and later employed by small-minded roommates.

( ) An unexciting but oddly satisfying activity necessary in moderate quantity for the reasonable enjoyment of a civilized home.

( ) One of life's most exalted pleasures and your chosen avocation, to be pursued with never-ending zeal and ruthless efficiency.

10. **Your attitudes toward household cleanliness are closest to which of the following types (please indicate with a check mark those specific traits you possess and mark the category in which you've checked the most traits):**

( ) TYPE A

____ You insist that the path from kitchen to bedroom to bath be kept reasonably clear at all times.

____ You view toothpaste buildup in the bathroom sink as an aesthetic plus.

____ You consider growing flourishing mold on the tile grout a form of gardening.

____ Like the Hindus, you believe that it is wrong to harm any living thing, including cockroaches. (Are you Hindu?_____)

____ Thanks to underpowered olfactory glands, you are blissfully oblivious to garbage odors—even in July.

____ Dirty socks make charming and creative Christmas tree ornaments.

____ Never washing or sweeping floors results in ever-changing and developing color patterns that enhance décor and lend a natural feeling underfoot.

____ You harvest the living room rug annually.

____ An undefrosted refrigerator makes every trip to the freezer an Arctic expedition, and affords you the chance to use ice axes and pitons to remove food.

____ Huge dust devils inspire romantic notions about "tumblin' tumbleweed."

____ Dirty dishes lend a homey feel to your environment, and dirty pots and pans offer a particularly tender air of domesticity. Besides, having no clean dishes on hand can be an aid to dieting, and allows you to take inventory of the china easily.

( ) TYPE B

____ Your nickname is Isopropyl.

_____ You sterilize cotton balls before you use them, boil your toothbrush daily, and like to see your reflection in woodwork.

_____ You wash dishes before and after you use them.

_____ You budget 10 percent of your salary for Comet, Mr. Clean, Spic and Span and Lysol (Regular and Basin, Tub and Tile Cleaner).

_____ You have been hospitalized with damaged lungs as a result of combining large quantities of chlorine bleach and ammonia while cleaning the bathroom.

_____ You send the plastic shower curtain out to be dry cleaned, iron bath towels, and spend so much time with your Hoover that some suspect unnatural affinities.

_____ You buy Easy-Off by the case, and consider all perishable goods expendable when they interfere with the defrost cycle.

_____ You carry a damp cloth in a plastic baggie at all times, just in case of a spill.

_____ You consider baseboard cleaning methods a suitable topic for cocktail party conversation.

_____ The only items you will permit to be left lying around are:
1. Today's newspaper (in newsstand-fresh condition, centered perfectly on the coffee table).
2. The glass of water your roommate or guest is still drinking (on a coaster and centered perfectly on the coffee table).

_____ You define "still drinking" as at least one sip per minute.

( ) TYPE C

_____ You are reasonable, flexible, moderate.

Reread carefully the traits and your selections in Types A and B above. (Warning: Most people who are really Type A or Type B feel that they are Type C.)

RELIGIONS

11. **Are you a member of any organized religious group?**

( ) Yes   ( ) No

If yes, do you plan to host in the home a religious meeting, revival, prayer circle, rally, retreat, encounter group, séance, assembly, convention, convocation, gathering or other get-together function?_____

_____

12. **Do your religious beliefs interfere in any way with the control of household pests by either chemicals or physical force?**

( ) Yes   ( ) No

If yes, what are the restrictions?_____
List pests._____

CULTURAL PREFERENCES

13. **Music:**

    ( ) LIVE   ( ) RECORDED

    If live, alone or in groups?_____

    TYPE:

    ( ) Jazz   ( ) Rock   ( ) Classical   ( ) Country & Western
    ( ) Folk   ( ) Reggae   ( ) Serious modern   ( ) Opera
    ( ) Conceptual   ( ) Bagpipe   ( ) MOR   ( ) New Wave
    ( ) Show tunes   ( ) Indian exotic   ( ) Whaling chanteys
    ( ) Gamelan   ( ) Other

    If other, please describe._____

    _____

14. **Do you ever play any one record more than three times per day?**

    ( ) Yes   ( ) No

15. **Do you own headphones?**

    ( ) Yes   ( ) No

    If yes, do you use them upon request?_____

    If no, check the closest description of the volume level at which you like to listen:

    _____ Barely audible above a whisper—just for background.

    _____ Moderate volume—conversation can be conducted easily.

    _____ Loud, frankly, but not too disturbing when door is shut and bass is held in check.

    _____ Definitely distracting to roommate(s) and probably to neighbors.

    _____ "I feel the earth move under my feet . . ."

16. **Whistling:**

    ( ) Yes   ( ) No

    If yes, where?_____

    ( ) a happy tune   ( ) while you work

OTHER

17. **Do you sell Tupperware?**

    ( ) Yes   ( ) No

    If yes, do you get discounts for roommates?_____

    How much would a complete set run me?_____

18. **Hobbies:**
    ( ) Stamp collecting   ( ) Belly dancing   ( ) Baton twirling
    ( ) Snow sculpture   ( ) Other
    If yes to snow sculpture, please see question 19.

19. **Drugs:**
    Do you use them?
    ( ) Yes   ( ) No
    Do you sell them?
    ( ) Yes   ( ) No
    If yes, what kind of unregistered gun do you own?_____
    If yes, does the following statement apply: "If it's white and on the table, I snort it."_____

    A ROACH IS:
    ( ) A disgusting insect that should be banished from human living quarters.
    ( ) A toy and food supplement for cats.
    ( ) A curved cut in the edge of a sail. (Does your yacht club allow guests?)
    ( ) The unsmoked end of a marijuana cigarette.

    COKE IS:
    ( ) Short for Coca-Cola.
    ( ) It.
    ( ) Coal residue produced by the steel-making process. (Are you from W.VA.?)
    ( ) Slang for cocaine.

    SPEED IS:
    ( ) An expression of velocity.
    ( ) A sensation of rushing motion that many people like.
    ( ) Of the essence.
    ( ) A stimulant.

    DOWNS ARE:
    ( ) Elevator buttons.
    ( ) Race courses for horses. (You're probably the same one who answered the roach question as part of a sail.)
    ( ) The things they fill vests with.
    ( ) Depressants.

20. **Are you an ax murderer?**
    ( ) Yes   ( ) No
    Really?_____

LEAVING THINGS AROUND

Conflict between two roommates can arise because of an insidious habit one or both may possess: LEAVING THINGS AROUND—also known as LEAVING THINGS LYING AROUND.

If one roommate is a neatnik and the other a slob, the problem is simply solved.

The slob will be the one leaving things around and the neatnik will either continually pick up after the slob, move or force the slob to move.

The real danger of leaving things around occurs when two relatively neat people or two slobs live together.

CASE HISTORY 1

Bud and Jack are old friends and young professionals living in Minneapolis. Neither has quite gotten over college living habits.

Jack never puts the dishes in the sink, and they lie around just about everywhere. Bud puts the dishes in the sink but never washes them.

The coffee cup with the beginnings of a new wonder drug at the bottom and the plates bearing last Thursday's spaghetti are perched on the TV.

Other grungy pieces of china rest upon the little table in the hall, where Bud and Jack used to put the mail until the avocado soldered itself to Bud's tax refund.

Identifying the remains on the dishes under Jack's bed would require Carbon 14 dating.

Bud, who has a closet organized into two large piles—one clean and unironed, one dirty and unironed—is by no means a clean freak.

But when he and Jack were almost evicted because the rent bill was lost under a Swanson frozen pie plate lying under the couch, he decided to take action.

He called Jack at work. Jack was distraught to find he had misplaced that evening's invitation to the gallery opening at which he had intended to woo Kathy into a meaningful relationship.

At that moment, Bud spied the invitation peeking out from the top of a half-eaten box of Ritz crackers. He offered to bring it over to Jack if Jack would have drinks with him immediately following work. Over stiff G&Ts, Bud and Jack agreed that the apartment had become unmanageable.

They spent the entire next weekend organizing and cleaning, finding things they thought had been lost forever.

Bud discovered the gold Dunhill lighter his father had given him. When his Dad asked him why he used a Bic, he would say, "I save it for dressy occasions."

Jack found the phone number of a girl he had met in Bermuda stuck to the side of a Häagen-Dazs ice cream container.

After their two-day cleaning session, Bud and Jack sat back, admired their efforts, and went out to celebrate at the local bar. After much self-congratulation, Jack noted it was time to go home and change for their Sunday night dates.

When they got to the apartment door, Jack turned to Bud and asked, "Do you have the keys?"

"No," Bud replied. "I left them on that hook we put up so we wouldn't lose them."

CASE HISTORY 2

Ted and Ian are business associates at a Big Eight firm in New York City. Both dress impeccably, and their entire East Side apartment is pristine. The rooms embody the old saw, "A place for everything and everything in its place."

Nevertheless, there are problems in paradise.

It takes Ted and Ian between three and four hours just to get out of the house in the morning.

At breakfast, each knife, fork, spoon, plate and egg cup must be cleaned immediately after use and placed in the slotted Rubbermaid drainer. Once Ian cleaned out Ted's pan of scrambled eggs before they were finished cooking.

A shower and a shave take only half an hour, but scrubbing the tub and sink runs forty-five minutes.

Ted and Ian rarely arrive at the office before noon, and so must work late into the night.

No one will come to Ted and Ian's parties if anything more than an appetizer is being served. They can't stand the two-hour wait between courses.

Once Ted cleared out the guests at his own birthday party by handing out the three hundred coasters he owns, plus individual ashtrays.

After losing their jobs and friends, Ted and Ian decided to hire a maid. Now it takes only the weekend to clean up after her.

In the Shrill of the Night:
Roommates Respond to Crisis

The following multiple-choice questionnaire was devised to help you assess your ability to cope with a number of potential crisis situations. It should also be filled out by your roommate(s) to gauge compatibility in handling trouble. It will help you determine, too, the likelihood of your residence surviving any or all of these emergencies.

1. It's 3:00 A.M. Your roommate has roused you from a sound sleep. She is standing over your bed, tears streaming down her cheeks, holding a meat cleaver. You ask:
   a). Am I having a nightmare?
   b). Are you and Roger fighting?
   c). Have you finally decided to enroll at the culinary institute?
   d). Is there someone in the apartment?
   e). Have I upset you in any way?

2. Your roommate comes home in tattered clothing, wearing only one shoe, escorted by two police officers. You ask:
   a). Rough day at work?
   b). Rusty's leash break again?
   c). You didn't shoot Roger, did you?
   d). Were you mugged?

3. Your roommate claims there have been voices outside your bedroom window. You find this unlikely because you live on the tenth floor of an apartment building. You ask:
   a). Are you still reading my copy of *I Never Promised You a Rose Garden?*
   b). Have they fixed the fire escape?
   c). Could it be the neighbors' TV?
   d). That coke is really something, huh?

4. You come home to find your roommate agitated to the point of speechlessness and pointing to the empty TV table. You ask:
   a). Nothing good on tonight?
   b). Think the table needs refinishing?
   c). Have we been robbed?
   d). Have I upset you in any way?

5. Your roommate bangs the receiver onto the phone cradle and screams disjointed words and phrases, such as "Over," "Finished," "We're through," "Trusted the louse," and "What's left?" You ask:
   a). Wrong number?
   b). Are we still doubling Friday night?

c). If you're finished, may I make a call?

d). Have I upset you in any way?

6. You smell smoke, trace it to the kitchen, and there see your roommate flapping a dish towel at flames leaping wildly from the stove top. You ask:

a). New recipe?

b). Remember, I like mine rare?

c). Should I call the fire department?

d). Want me to set the table?

7. Your roommate explains that a registered letter has just been delivered containing an eviction notice. You've no case to contest the suit. You ask:

a). Did you ask the guy in for coffee?

b). Suppose we should wait to paint the bathroom?

c). Oh, well, did he bring my UPS package for that new bomber plane model?

d). Well, maybe we should start looking for a new place?

NOT COMING HOME: WHEN ROOMMATES WORRY

The lives of roommates become intertwined. This is unavoidable. When answering a phone call for a roommate, few people will claim not to know what city their roommate is in, or what he or she does for a living, or deny that a person by that name lives there.

But given the speed with which we live our lives, and the resulting complexity, there are occasions when the whereabouts of a roommate is in question, and in some cases the identity of the roommate is in question as well.

Some roommates remedy this uncertainty by informing their co-habitors as to locale, time, and temp every twenty minutes or so.

"I'm leaving work now, going to pick up my laundry and might even buy a new pair of running shoes. Need anything at the store? I should be home at 5:45, if not sooner."

But most roommates fall into one of the three following categories:

THE LAISSEZ-FAIRE ROOMMATE

Jan is a laissez-faire roommate. She figures Buffy can take care of herself. Besides, if she wanted to worry about somebody, she'd get married and have a kid.

So when Buffy disappears for three weeks, Jan doesn't bat an eye. She figures Buffy met some guy and took off for a romp in the Caribbean.

When Buffy finally returns home, Jan calmly relates that they have been receiving some strange-sounding phone calls lately. Buffy just as calmly informs Jan that the kidnapers always covered the receiver with a handkerchief.

THE CROCK POT ROOMMATE

Sally has known Guy only for a short time, but he seems like a nice enough person, and the roommate service provided her with plenty of evidence of his stability and good character.

Guy, who is playing in a country club tennis tourney this weekend, asks her if she'd like to attend a match or two. Sally is delighted. He'll drive her out on Saturday morning.

But Saturday morning comes with no call from Guy. Sally hangs around the apartment and waits by the phone.

A little worried but mostly annoyed, she cancels her date for the evening and begins to steam. By the time she cancels Sunday brunch, she is boiling.

When Guy hits the door Monday morning with a few days' stubble and a hangover advertising his defeat in the tourney Friday afternoon, Sally really explodes. Guy can't convince her she shouldn't have stewed.

THE NATIONAL GUARD ROOMMATE

Mike and Don grew up together in Scarsdale, attended NYU, and stayed in New York to pursue careers. Mike adjusted well to the city, keeping up an active social life.

But Don spent more and more time at home. He let his imagination dwell on all the terrible things he read about in the New York *Post,* and he worried about Mike's welfare.

One evening, Mike didn't come home.

Against his better instincts, Don went to sleep anyway. He woke up at 6:00 A.M. and saw that Mike was not in his bed.

Don got out Mike's address book and placed thirty or forty calls before he really panicked. He phoned the local precinct and was just about to say what Mike was last seen wearing, when Mike came through the front door looking very weary and very happy.

Mike appreciated Don's concern, although he thought it a little excessive. Mike and Don decided to set up a system.

Now, if either of them thinks he may be out all night, he will call the other and say (so as not to be obvious to his date), "Moriarty's biscuits are rotting in a rusty scupper."

For WHOM THE BELL TOLLS

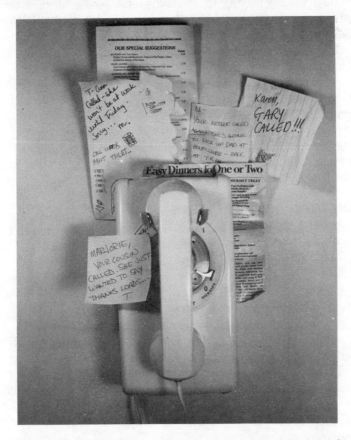

One of the greatest sources of conflict among roommates is a device which rings and rings and rings in the middle of the night, and when you have groggily grabbed it by the throat and mumbled hello, you find it's for your roommate who is on a camping trip in Wyoming.

Yes, the phone. It sends you a bill every month, it doesn't properly activate the answering machine, it rings once and stops, and it allows you to hear someone from Spokane better than someone across town. Whether you have one phone in your flat or five in your studio apartment, you are slave, not master, to the instrument. Every so often you must use vacation days to wait for the repairman to come fix the light on the princess phone or change the cord which the dog has chewed. Although you may have had a marvelous relationship with your roommates for the past two years, you will never speak to them again if they don't tell you that Bill/Sue called, offering you a ticket to the Stones concert. Worst of all, each month you must allot four hours of intensive study to decipher the bill and decide who pays what. (For this you should hire an accountant or take a CPA course yourself and purchase a calculator that does square roots.)

Karen, Marjorie, and Tracy are three New York roommates whose annotated phone bill reveals much about their lives—and, incidentally, their telephone habits.

KEY TO LONG-DISTANCE PHONE BILL

1). Karen calls West Coast love Gary. He won't move back to New York as long as film project is viable. Karen threatens to break things off—wants him to forget screenwriting, resume budding career as stockbroker. Karen hears female giggling in background, threatens to commit suicide. Gary says it's the TV. Karen makes mental note to call Los Angeles TV stations to see if any comedies were on that night. They make up—cooing on both ends.

2). Karen insists Gary return to New York in three weeks. Heated conversation ensues: Every transgression of two-year relationship is iterated; recriminations, threats and vows never to speak to each other again.

3). Marjorie calls mother in Tampa. Dad still playing golf and Mom fixing dinner. Rundown of events from Marjorie. New boyfriend, job a drag, new Neil Simon play with friends that evening. Finds out brother thinking of quitting law school to raise exotic trees in Australia. Mom distraught but . . . Dad just walked in. Marjorie does not tell Mom about plans to spend weekend with new boss. Says she will write, but most likely will call.

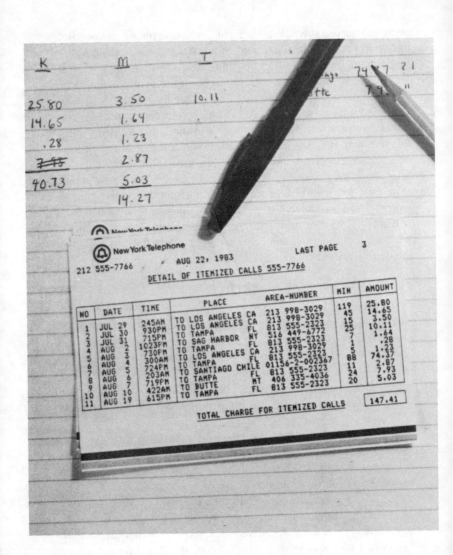

4). Tracy calls workmate Ann at summer house. Why didn't she come to work on Monday? Everyone at the agency is furious—Ann's big project was due. Tracy did most of it, just got home. She'll be at the office another five hours tomorrow night to finish her own work. Decides to really tell Ann off, sever relations. Who cares if Ann was the only one Tracy could count on in a pinch?

Ann answers phone in a daze. Music blares in background. Ann getting over tragic love affair. Can't imagine putting on jeans or brushing teeth, much less going to work. Tracy agrees to cook up story for their boss. Tells Ann to take a couple of days off; she will cover. Tracy gets off phone, feels like a fool.

5). Marjorie hears rumor about old high school pal getting married. Can't imagine to whom. Calls Mom for verification and more info.

6). Karen can't sleep, calls Gary. What the hell, he's still the best thing she's run across in years. Female voice answers. Karen wakes up Tracy. They drain a bottle of cheap Scotch, go to work with hangovers the next day.

7). Did new driver's license arrive? Please send to NY pronto.

8). Fred from Marjorie's office gets very drunk at party, remembers young woman from Chile he met at Empire State Building. Promised he would call one day, might as well do it now. Karen, Tracy and Marjorie never figure this one out, accuse each other's friends of having made call, end up splitting cost.

9). Marjorie starts new diet. Calls Mom to compare notes. What are you having for dinner?

10). Not the night of a party. No one knows anyone in Butte. After Tracy makes three calls to billing-inquiries number, phone company agrees this is a mistake. To be credited on next bill.

11). Marjorie has terrible day at the office. Snubbed by new trainee. Bad cold for the past three days. What's that recipe for chicken soup? How's Dad's golf game?

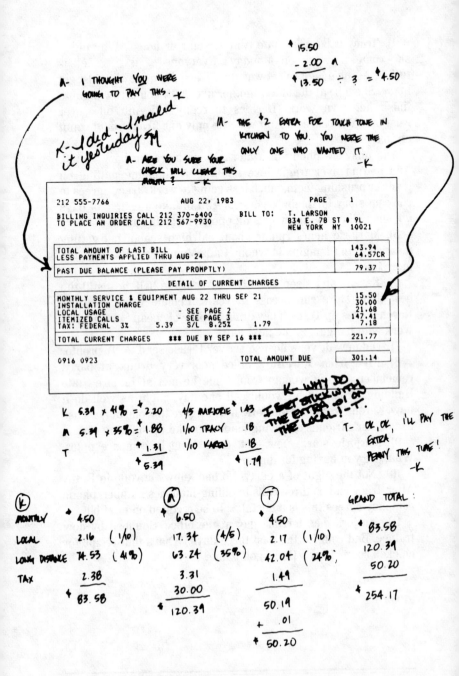

$15.50
-2.00 A
$13.50 \div 3 = 4.50

A- I THOUGHT YOU WERE GOING TO PAY THIS. -K

K- I did I mailed it yesterday -M

A- ARE YOU SURE YOUR CHECK WILL CLEAR THIS MONTH? -K

1A- THE $2 EXTRA FOR TOUCH TONE IN KITCHEN TO YOU. YOU WERE THE ONLY ONE WHO WANTED IT. -K

```
212 555-7766              AUG 22, 1983              PAGE    1

BILLING INQUIRIES CALL 212 370-6400    BILL TO:   T. LARSON
TO PLACE AN ORDER CALL 212 567-9930               834 E. 78 ST # 9L
                                                  NEW YORK  NY  10021

┌─────────────────────────────────────────────────────────────┬──────────┐
│ TOTAL AMOUNT OF LAST BILL                                     │  143.94  │
│ LESS PAYMENTS APPLIED THRU AUG 24                             │  64.57CR │
├─────────────────────────────────────────────────────────────┼──────────┤
│ PAST DUE BALANCE (PLEASE PAY PROMPTLY)                        │   79.37  │
└─────────────────────────────────────────────────────────────┴──────────┘

                     DETAIL OF CURRENT CHARGES

┌─────────────────────────────────────────────────────────────┬──────────┐
│ MONTHLY SERVICE & EQUIPMENT AUG 22 THRU SEP 21               │   15.50  │
│ INSTALLATION CHARGE                                          │   30.00  │
│ LOCAL USAGE          - SEE PAGE 2                            │   21.68  │
│ ITEMIZED CALLS       - SEE PAGE 3                            │  147.41  │
│ TAX: FEDERAL 3%    5.39    S/L 8.25%      1.79              │    7.18  │
├─────────────────────────────────────────────────────────────┼──────────┤
│ TOTAL CURRENT CHARGES    *** DUE BY SEP 16 ***              │  221.77  │
└─────────────────────────────────────────────────────────────┴──────────┘

0916 0923                         TOTAL AMOUNT DUE    │  301.14  │
```

K $5.39 \times 41\% = 2.20 4/5 MARJORIE $1.43

A $5.39 \times 35\% = 1.88 1/10 TRACY   .18

T $1.31   1/10 KAREN   .18
                  $5.39 $1.79

K- WHY DO I GET STUCK WITH THE EXTRA $.01 ON THE LOCAL! -T

T- OK, OK, I'LL PAY THE EXTRA PENNY THIS TIME! -K

Ⓚ		Ⓐ		Ⓣ		GRAND TOTAL:
MONTHLY	$4.50	$6.50		$4.50		$83.58
LOCAL	2.16 (1/10)	17.34 (4/5)		2.17 (1/10)		120.39
LONG DISTANCE	74.53 (41%)	63.24 (35%)		42.04 (24%)		50.20
TAX	2.38	3.31		1.49		$254.17
	$83.58	30.00		50.19		
		$120.39		+ .01		
				$50.20		

A&T - I WON'T BE PAYING LOCAL
USAGE AFTER THIS MONTH.
I MAKE ALL MY LOCAL CALLS
FROM THE OFFICE
              -K

K- Then stop calling
time, weather information
and horoscope. Do you
think these calls
are FREE nitwit?
                    M

212 555-7766   AUG 22, 1983   PAGE   2

DETAIL OF LOCAL USAGE

CALL AREA	CALL RATE*	ADDL MIN RATE	8AM-9PM NO DISCOUNT		9PM-11PM# 35% DISCOUNT		11PM-8AM## 60% DISCOUNT		
			CALLS	ADDL MINS	CALLS	ADDL MINS	CALLS	ADDL MINS	AMOUNT
A	9.0c	-	240	-	31	-	42	-	25.68
B	11.0c	3.0c	0	0	0	0	0	0	0.00
CHARGES				21.60		1.81		2.27	25.68

LESS USAGE ALLOWANCE   4.00

TOTAL LOCAL USAGE CHARGE   21.68

*Area A rate is per call.
#Also 5PM-11PM Sun & holidays.
##Also 8AM Sat-5PM Sun.

T- CAN WE GET A LOWER
RATE OR SOMETHING?
WE NEVER CALL OUTSIDE
MANHATTAN. -K

K&M - WOULD YOU
MIND STAYING
OFF THE PHONE ON
WEDS. BTW. 11:00 & 11:15 PM
THAT'S WHEN MOM LIKES
TO CALL. THANKS.
                T.

M- YOUR COUSIN FROM SANTA FE
RAN THIS UP 5 TIMES
HIGHER THAN NORMAL.
YOU PAY 4/5.
                -K

"WE'RE NOT HOME RIGHT NOW": The Answering Machine

The answering machine has become indispensable in today's society, even for roommates. After all, there are still times when no one's home, and you wouldn't want to miss any important messages. What should be a convenience can easily become a bone of contention, however, because you and your roommate must decide what sort of outgoing message to leave. There are three basic types.

1). Your roommate leaves the outgoing message:

"Hi. This is Zeke. I'm not home right now. You can try me at the office, or at Sarah's, or leave a message at the club. Oh, Josh isn't home either."

2). You both leave the outgoing message:

ZEKE: "Hi, this is Zeke."
JOSH: "Hi, this is Josh."
TOGETHER: "You guessed it. We're not home right now. We've gone out . . ."
ZEKE (in Humphrey Bogart voice): ". . . to find the Maltese Falcon."
JOSH (in Groucho Marx voice): ". . . for A Day at the Races."
TOGETHER: "We won't be back until we . . ."
ZEKE: ". . . climb the High Sierra."
JOSH: ". . . make Duck Soup."
TOGETHER: "So leave your name, number and the time you called, and we'll get back to you . . ."
ZEKE: ". . . sweetheart."
JOSH: ". . . if we don't get back at you first."

3). You leave the outgoing message:

"Hi. This is Josh. I'm not home. If you want to leave a message for me, I'll get back to you as soon as I can. If you called last week, you know where Zeke is. Bye."

PLEASE RE-LEASE ME

Unless you are a squatter or some other form of social parasite, you most likely have some form of legal document to protect your living space—a lease if you rent or a deed if you own your habitat. Most of those in roommateland are lessees rather than deedees.

The lease is a contract fraught with ethical as well as legal implications. For instance, if you and your roommate sign a lease for an apartment together, you both have a legal right to occupy that living space, as well as ethical responsibilities for each other's comfort and well-being.

If only one of you is on the lease (a frequent occurrence, especially in big cities with a highly mobile population of roommates), the leaseholder has considerably more power than the roommate whose name is not on the lease. The lease-holding roommate also has many more options, since in most cities it is very hard to find a desirable apartment at a reasonable price. It is hoped that a person wielding such great power will exercise it reasonably and with care, but as the old saying goes, "Power corrupts and absolute power . . ."

The following are some guidelines for the lease-holding roommate to prevent unintentional unethical behavior toward the non-lease-holding roommate.

It is not acceptable either to reprimand or expel your roommate for:

- Not offering to do your laundry even though she is throwing in a load herself.
- Not introducing you to the new gentleman she has been seeing, or any of his cute friends.
- Not cleaning up the kitchen after your dinner party, even though she knows you have to get up early in the morning.
- Not inviting you along on that great Caribbean vacation she took with her friends.

- Not listening to your trials and tribulations at work, in love, about your family, etc., when she is getting ready to go to work in the morning and is already running a few minutes late.
- Not letting you hook up your speakers to her stereo system, even if it would give you both "music in every room."
- Not lending you $500 for that terrific dress you saw the other day or not paying for the entire phone bill, since she uses it more often than you do anyway.
- Not taking your mother around town while you are at work, even though you know she has loads of vacation time coming.
- Not letting you come home with her for Christmas, even if her family lives much closer than yours and all that air fare saved would come in really handy.
- Not waiting up for you to come home from a date with George, to help fend him off when he makes his usual pass.
- Asking why you go out with George anyway.

THE ROOMMATE GENEALOGY

Mark, Bill and Ken graduate from Purdue together and decide to take a three-bedroom apartment in the Lincoln Park section of Chicago.

Mark takes acting classes and spends much of his time away from the apartment. Bill has his girlfriend, Phyllis, over four out of seven nights a week.

Tom, Mark's friend from acting class, crashes in Mark's room since his building is going condo. Tom agrees to pay one-sixth of the rent.

Bill's affair with Phyllis reaches the boiling point and she moves in.

Mark meets a girl named Susan at the bus stop and two weeks later convinces her to move in with him. Susan will not be paying rent. Tom will move to the living room couch. Tom objects, but his name is not on the lease.

Ken, put off by the recent changes in living conditions and feeling stymied in his career as a novelist/night clerk at the Ambassador, decides to go off to graduate school.

Susan's friend Martha from Oregon is dying to take a shot at acting. Susan convinces Mark to let Martha move in and take Ken's room. Tom objects, but his name is not on the lease.

Martha insists she is looking for her own place but stays on and on.

Bill hears of a great loft in HuSu they can all get if they move fast. Everyone packs the entire contents of apartment and gets ready to move.

Loft deal falls through. Unpack.

Phyllis and Martha do not get along. This leads to a terrible fight between Bill and Mark, then between Susan and Mark.

Susan moves out. Tom moves back into Mark's room.

Mark and Martha hit it off, decide to get married, and move to their own apartment in Rogers Park. Tom finally gets his own room.

Evan, Tom's brother from Portage, Wisconsin, takes over Martha's old room.

As Bill and Phyllis wind down their relationship, Phyllis has a nervous breakdown. She returns home to California.

Anything to do with the apartment reminds Bill of Phyllis. He splits without a word or a forwarding address.

Bill leaves behind a long-distance bill that will take several years for former roommates to pay off. Tom coordinates the cross-country collection effort.

Evan meets Cindy at work and asks her to move in.

Winter comes and there is no heat or hot water. Nobody objects.

Nobody's name is on the lease.

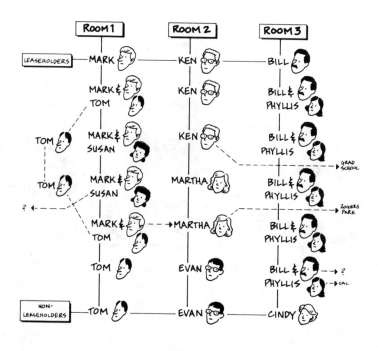

THE SLOW BURN *or* I'VE GOT YOU UNDER MY SKIN

It is inevitable that from time to time you will get on your roommate's nerves. This is only truly dangerous if you have decided irrevocably to remove yourself or your roommate from the premises—legally or not.

Generally, though, you will get on each other's nerves for just a short period of time. Then the roommate whose nerves you are on blows up, apologizes for blowing up, and you swear undying loyalty to each other and laugh about how silly you've been acting.

HOW TO TELL IF YOU ARE GETTING ON YOUR ROOMMATE'S NERVES

1). Innocent inquiries are greeted with heavy sarcasm. For example:

YOU: "I picked up the mail and left it on the hall table."

ROOMMATE: "Great, after you're done reading mine, perhaps you would like to go through my desk drawer."

2). You make their favorite snack and they won't eat it.

3). You ask them if they have change for a dollar and they glare at you as if you had just asked for an option on their firstborn child.

4). They are suddenly very concerned about dishes in the kitchen sink and unemptied wastebaskets.

5). They go directly to their room after work and come out only to fix dinner, which they then retire to their room with, giving the door a smart slam.

6). They answer the phone, put the receiver down and walk away from it, forgetting to tell you it's for you.

7). They tell everybody who calls that you are not home even though you are only in the bathroom.

8). They stop passing along *Time* and *People* after they are through reading them.

9). They refuse all your invitations, saying they have something better to do.

10). They begin referring to you as "only" their roommate, as in "Mary? Oh, that's *only* my roommate."

HEART TO HEART:
Telling Your Roommate Off

Most roommate relationships exist in a state of truce. It is not that some of your roommates behavior doesn't bother you; it's just that it isn't worth the time or trouble or the possibility of losing a basically good roommate to detail the little shortcomings and character flaws of someone who helps you pay the rent. And, God knows, there are plenty of ax murderers and other pathological types out there, ready to take your roommate's place should he take exception to your gentle efforts in his interest.

But there is another reason you must exercise great caution when you decide enough is enough and the time has come to lay it on the line. You have to be ready to deal with that special brand of logic that roommates seem to be born with.

BOB: "Listen, Ted, I think it is very important that we talk. There is something that is really bothering me."

TED: "Shoot, Bob."

BOB: "Well, here it is the second week of the month and you still haven't come across with the rent. And it's not like this is the first time, either. I am constantly using my money to write the landlord a check and then spend the next two weeks trying to get the money from you. I ought to start charging interest."

TED: "Well, Bob, I thought I explained to you that I was saving up to buy a new set of sparkplugs for my motorcycle and that I would be a little late this month. By the way, don't you owe me a few dollars from something?"

BOB: "What! Oh. Yeah. I guess I do owe you for the New Year's Eve party. How much was that?"

TED: "About a hundred ought to do it. Let's see, at 11 percent interest for six months . . ."

BOB: "Eleven percent!"

TED: "That's prime, buddy."

BOB: "Well, you can just take off for every time you borrowed my blue suit. I figure twenty bucks a rental. Three rentals . . ."

TED: "Okay, you want to play that game? I think that at least three nights a week, I make dinner . . ."

BOB: "If you want to call it that."

TED: ". . . and at average caterer's prices that would be about . . ."

BOB: "Yeah, well, don't forget to divide that by the number of times your girlfriend eats over here."

TED: "Okay, minus what Joan eats . . ."

BOB: "All right, all right! This is getting out of hand. Just get the rent to me as soon as you can."

TED: "Sure thing. What about my hundred bucks?"

Ten Reasons to End
A Roommate Relationship

1). You return home after a week's vacation and your toothbrush is wet.

2). The clasp on your diary has been tampered with.

3). Your cat "accidentally" falls out of a tenth-story window while home alone with your roommate, who has loudly expressed dislike for cats on several occasions.

4). Your roommate develops a phone friendship with your parents that goes far beyond the bounds of pleasantry or politeness. When they call, your roommate doesn't announce it. Instead, he or she tells them everything you'd planned to say, as well as everything you'd planned not to say. Ten minutes into the call comes the summons, "It's your parents . . ."

5). Your roommate views you as a private dating service, feels free to pursue any of your romantic leads.

6). Your roommate offers your boyfriend or girlfriend little confidences about you: "He always takes forever in the shower," or, "She only wears red underwear when you're around," etc.

7). Despite repeated requests, your roommate "just can't help" consuming your favorite, specially purchased grocery items. Roommate never replaces these foods and certainly never buys them to share with you.

8). The amount of money your roommate owes you at any given time exceeds 10 percent of your annual income.

9). For women only: Your roommate borrows your diaphragm. Worse: Your roommate borrows your diaphragm for his girlfriend to use.

10). For men only: Your roommate's girlfriend uses your razor to shave her legs. Then she puts the razor in her makeup case and zips case shut.

FAMILIARITY BREEDS...

FALLING IN LOVE WITH YOUR ROOMMATE

Enlightened twentieth-century people, transformed by the sexual revolution and women's liberation, now know that men and women must treat each other as human beings first and sex objects not at all. It is now accepted that both men and women can have platonic friends of the opposite sex. This has led legions of roommates to conclude that living with a member of the opposite sex without a romantic attachment is not only possible but desirable.

Of course, like much enlightened thinking, these appealing notions rarely work in real-life contexts. If you do start regarding your opposite-sex roommate with more than mere friendliness, the following pros and cons should be kept in mind.

PROS

It is not necessary to place a phone call to make a date.

It is not necessary to put on airs. Anyone who shares a bathroom with you already knows your medical and social history from looking in the medicine cabinet. They know your likes, your dislikes and your little quirks. If they are still living with you of their own volition, you have eliminated 99 percent of the things that would traditionally keep someone from falling in love with you.

It is not necessary to inquire "Your place or mine?"

It is not necessary to inquire "Do you have to work in the morning?," since you know their schedule better than your own.

It is not necessary to dress for dinner.

It is not necessary to call a cab or put on your coat and go and hunt for one at 4:00 A.M.

It is not necessary to inquire about other relationships. After a few weeks you are both pretty sure of what's going on in each other's lives.

It is not necessary to call the next day and explain that you two are "ships passing in the night," since you will pass each other three thousand times in the upcoming week.

It is not necessary to call the next day to reaffirm your interest in the other party. Making breakfast together should be affirmation enough.

It is not necessary to explain the relationship to friends, parents, neighbors or workmates. "We share an apartment" is nicely ambiguous and covers all possibilities.

It is not necessary to worry about which part of town to see a movie or eat in, since you both live in the same neighborhood.

CONS

If you have made a mistake you will have to face it, like the sun rising in the east, like the alarm going off in the morning.

The period of "true romance" will be greatly shortened by your living together. Once you have become more than roommates, there will be no secrets left. You already know about the dishes left perpetually in the sink and the wet towel on the bathroom floor.

One of the wonderful things about a new love interest is getting to know a new apartment. This you have already done.

If you break up and decide to be "adult" about things and continue sharing living space after the affair is over, you have several interesting situations to look forward to.

First, those little "quirks" that were so easy to overlook before—like the asparagus juice which seems to inundate all contents of the refrigerator—now have you constantly on edge.

Then the appearance of a new love interest, which puts you right back in the role of "just a roommate," tries your patience and goodwill constantly.

Next, a loving make-up note is slipped gently under your door so that your own new love interest can find it on the way to the bathroom the next morning.

Your practical, household-problem-solving discussions with your roommate make it sound like you two have been married for twenty years rather than living together for two months.

The awful reality will dawn on you: If you have a really serious falling out, there is more at stake than a broken heart. Much more: A broken lease, and you know you will never find another apartment at this price. Then you realize someone will be moving, usually you, and you will face the only thing worse than losing a loved one. Losing a beloved apartment.

4

A ROOM OF ONE'S OWN: By Yourself with Others

Sometimes a person decides that he or she wants to live "by myself." According to the theory of interdependence, this is really just an indirect way of describing your roommate relationship.

What about roaches?

What about the moans, groans, footsteps, slamming doors and shrieking tires of your neighbors?

What about your answering machine? So what if most of your calls are messages from your plumber, last-minute cancellations and resounding clicks from people who refuse to talk to machines?

And what about all those friends, relatives and best-friend's-college-roommate's-second-cousin-from-Des-Moines types you're always inviting to stay with you because it's "no bother" and you "have the space"?

Sorry, nice try, but you're a roommate.

ALL BY MYSELF

People frequently find comfort in the thought of being alone—truly alone—and they even believe they can achieve this solitary bliss by renting their own apartment. Although delusions always die hard, they die hard quickly for single leaseholders.

Take Joan, for instance. Thrilled at finding her very own apartment—small, but sunny—she quickly settled accounts with her old roommates and jumped into the move.

And wasn't Joan's new next-door neighbor Sally kind to come by at 7:30 the next morning (Sunday) with coffee and doughnuts?

And wasn't Sally conscientious in making sure to take down Joan's home and office numbers, just in case? And concerned, too, in calling both numbers at least twice daily?

And wasn't Sally watchful? Surely if Joan's newspaper remained on her doorstep past 10:00 A.M., people might think she was away and try to break in.

And wasn't Sally intuitive? When John came to visit Joan after being out of town for four weeks, Sally knew she should: 1). meet the guy; 2). go out for dinner to offer a "fresh face" to the company; and 3). warn the young lovers how romance can go awry. (After all, Sally's boyfriend had walked out on her.)

And wasn't Sally civic-minded? Surely Joan didn't mind being volunteered to serve as block association chairperson for the next five years, although she didn't know the block association existed until Sally told her she was now in charge.

And wasn't Sally surprised? She certainly didn't understand when Joan fled back to her roommates after only six weeks.

I'VE GROWN ACCUSTOMED TO YOUR PACE

There is no way to escape getting to know your neighbors. Whether in a big city, a suburb or a small town, you just can't avoid them.

You meet in the hallway, the parking lot, the elevator, at the pool, in the mailroom, mowing the lawn.

You get to know your neighbors indirectly, too—by the sound of their keys in the lock (jangly and rushed, or relaxed and sensual), by their footsteps (measured and confident, or skipping and immature) and by the magazines and newspapers they throw out.

If friendly, neighbors do favors for one another. If not, they studiously avoid the suspicious-looking strangers coming out of someone else's door carrying suitcases jammed with household goods.

Whatever your relationship with your neighbors, they almost always play a major role in your life.

ONE MAN'S CEILING
IS ANOTHER MAN'S FLOOR

There are certain neighbors you will never meet except under the following conditions:

Your bathtub overflows.

Their bathtub overflows.

They decide a room divider should be constructed floor to ceiling.

You decide a room divider should be constructed floor to ceiling.

You have a party and invite them.
They have a party and invite you.
You have a party and don't invite them.
They have a party and don't invite you.
They have noisy sex.
You have noisy sex.
They like disco and you like Perry Como.
You like tumbling exercises and they like to sleep.

5

LOVE'S LABORS LEASED: ROMANTIC COHABITATION

Many roommates eventually choose a special form of room-matehood, and their roommates have special names—husband, wife, lover. This is romantic roommatehood, and it is distinguished by unique forms of emotional blackmail.

Still, the same psychological principle applies as in any roommate relationship: The little things will drive you crazy faster than the big ones.

Hester may love George dearly, but if he keeps squeezing blackheads in front of the bathroom mirror with the door open, she will threaten to leave him.

Special skills are required to keep love *and* the kitchen floor shining bright in this roommate situation.

KEY EXCHANGE

Love is indeed a madness. We buy burglar alarms to warn us that intruders are around. We buy guns to protect us from unforeseen foes. We have $150 locks on our doors to keep people out. So why, at the first sign of affection, do we hand over our keys to a love interest without the slightest hesitation? Even when we know what the consequences may be?

The rationale for this absurd behavior is always water-tight.

"Well, Janey and I have been seeing each other now for three months. We just love to spend time together. I usually stop by her place after work, but we always end up at my place because it is actually closer to both our jobs, and, besides, Janey's roommate is a real pill. I mean that girl can lower the temperature with just a glance. I have a better stereo, and we both love to listen to music. Janey likes my apartment a lot since it also has a great view.

"Well, we both kept running into all sorts of scheduling problems, 'cause Janey would need to get into the apartment for a dress or her toothpaste or something, and I figured, hell, it's a lot easier just to get her a set of keys and let her come and go as she pleases."

Six months later:

"How can I get my keys back from Janey without calling the whole thing off? I mean, I still like her and all, but I need a little more privacy. I can't ever have a friend of the opposite sex over, 'cause old Janey comes tripping in and fixes me with that 'I caught you' look, even though nothing is going on. I don't have a single inch of closet space left to myself, and she is forever having people call her here. Just last week one of her friends asked me how I liked living in Janey's apartment, doesn't it have a great view? *Her apartment?!*"

Of course, hindsight is perfect 20/20 so here are a few helpful guidelines:

Don't give your keys to anyone you have known less than ten years (unless you are married to them).

Don't give your keys to someone just once and expect them to get used to not having their own set again.

If you have given your keys to someone and now want them back but don't know how to ask for them, change the locks on the door and explain that you got only one set from the locksmith. Promise to have another set made, "real soon."

Your Place or Mine?

Congratulations. The long delicate process of falling in love has culminated in your decision to share the same abode and now your troubles really begin. It is no longer simply a question of who has more space in his or her apartment or house. The decision to live together must now take into account two careers, geography, and habits built up over an entire young adulthood of living in an extension of college dormitory life.

In order to make the proper decision take the following simple test:

Each of you should add up the points next to those items that most accurately describe your living situation. The person with the most points will provide the "host" domicile for the couple.

LIVING QUARTERS STABILITY	*Points*
You own your own house	50
You own your own apartment	40
You have a 3-year lease	30
You have a 1-year lease	20
You own a Winnebago	10
You own a tent	0

BIG ENOUGH FOR TWO?	*Points*
You have a 2-bedroom apartment	20
You have a 1-bedroom apartment	10
You have a studio apartment	5
You live in a rooming house	0
You have a mansion	50
You own one of the 50 states	100

FROM YOUR LIVING QUARTERS YOU CAN SEE:

	Points
A wall	0
A street	3
A street with trees	4
A street named after your family	25
A golf course	10
A lake	10
100 acres (yours)	50

IF YOU MOVE YOU WILL HAVE TO QUIT YOUR JOB. YOU ARE:

	Points
A newspaper delivery boy	5
A newspaperman	10
A tree surgeon	5
A surgeon	50
A broker	40
A break dancer	1
A writer	0

IF YOU MOVE YOU CAN'T BRING YOUR:

	Points
Mercedes	50
Color television	10
VCR	15
Dog	25
Cat	30
Patio furniture	2
Mother	50
Mother-in-law	0

NIGHT AND DAY, YOU ARE THE ONE: HOW THINGS CHANGE AFTER YOU MOVE IN TOGETHER

You decided to live together because you didn't need a piece of paper to prove you love each other. Now you wish you had a signed and sealed agreement spelling it all out.

You must decide: Who gets the surprise trip to the emergency room after cleaning the Cuisinart?

Who gives suppositories to the cat?

Who replies to Uncle Harry's too-frequently-asked question, "So when are you two kids really going to settle down and tie the knot?"

The free and easy openness that you prized during the early days of your relationship has now lost its charm. You do not want to be told that leaving dirty laundry strewn throughout your house shows a creative nature—you just want your live-in to do things *your* way.

You discover that your lover, like the good Dr. Jekyll, has a Mr. Hyde side.

You were always bowled over by How Great She Looks. Now you know how she does it:

She spends half an hour each morning blow-drying her nails.

She's known at the health club as Diehard.

She plasters her face every night with green-brown goo that goes for $40 an ounce.

She never stays up past 11:00 P.M. for *anything*.

Dinner means saltines and bouillon.

In short, her life is a constant struggle against the ravages of Time, Calories, and You.

And the boyish, manic all-night dancer who literally made you jump for joy—where does he get all that energy and *joie de vivre?*

He requires sixteen to eighteen hours' sleep after every bender.

He favors no companions other than his Golden Retriever for three days after that.

Sometimes, if the differences between you are not too great, you can work things out. You both admit that you have been a little selfish and that compromise is in order.

In a moment of enlightenment or foolishness—you won't know which until much later—you decide to make a greater commitment.

You finally have a satisfactory answer to Uncle Harry's question.

6

MALICE DOESN'T LIVE HERE ANYMORE: Dealing with the Ex-Roommate

TO MOVE OR NOT TO MOVE? THE INDECISIVE ROOMMATE

Your roommate has been tempted by another job, another city or another apartment for a long time now. But the prospect of actually packing up and moving just doesn't appeal. She goes back and forth, from wishy to washy, and can't seem to make up her mind.

"The career opportunities in retailing are really better here, even though I'd get a quick promotion to hosiery buyer in East Overshoe," she frets.

"But what if Susan and I don't get along as roommates? I don't want to ruin our friendship," she continues.

"John's apartment is bigger than this one, and I'd have a study as well as a bedroom, but our kitchen is brand-new, and you know how I really love to cook," she whines.

Meanwhile, you've got plans of your own that you'd like to proceed with, like getting another roommate, or finally fixing the place up to *your* liking, or holding a good-riddance party. Just when the whole thing is beginning to drive you a little crazy, she finally decides to take the plunge. You may heave a sigh of relief and think your problems are over.

Unfortunately, all your roommate's doubts about moving haven't gone away; they've just taken a new form. Now she wants the best of both worlds.

Is your roommate afraid that the new city/lover/job won't work out? Then she'll want to stay on your lease and sublet. This severely limits your living options, of course, but it's a small price to pay for your ex-roommate's peace of mind. Isn't it?

Your roommate's new place short on storage space? Surely you don't mind keeping a few of her things in your ample closets. And you'll be around when it's convenient for her to pick up the odd item, won't you?

Has your roommate claimed most of the things you bought together as hers alone? Propose King Solomon's solution—chopping everything in half.

Roommate fall in love with your pet? Arrange visitation rights in exchange for cleaning litter boxes or doing pooper-scooper duty.

COLLECTING FROM YOUR EX-ROOMMATE, or THE BIG WRITE-OFF

It can be difficult collecting a roommate's fair share of rent and utilities even when she's around. After she blows town, it can be next to impossible.

The problem is that once a roommate has decided to leave, she begins to lose interest in her current living situation. Especially in the bills. Especially when they're not in her name.

Unfortunately, conflicts with other roommates over paying bills are what often prompt a roommate to move in the first place.

Some people take precautions to make sure their roommates pay up. But in a deteriorating relationship even the best-laid plans are likely to go astray.

Here is an action checklist of measures to take, as well as what to do when they fail.

1). Require all new roommates to put down a deposit for utilities bills. Try to be stern when they run short of cash their third month in town and ask if they can use the deposit to cover that month's bills. But in reality, as you and they both know, you don't have much choice.

2). The next month, ask them to pay the current bill plus one month in advance. But this throws off their budget and two months later they have no money for utilities again.

3). "Let's simplify things," you say. "Just get the money to me by the time the bill is due every month and that will be OK."

4). They are two weeks late with the money and you have to cover the whole bill. You are getting tired of asking for money, and they are tired of being asked for it.

5). Delinquent roommate is now chronically two months late with utilities payments. You announce you will begin charging interest.

6). Roommate announces she has found a new place in a different city, for which she began looking when you announced you were charging interest on unpaid bills. During the last month, she has made many secret long-distance phone calls to arrange the move.

7). Roommate has moved. You get phone bill for $387.25, which includes not only her long-distance calls, but those of her boyfriend, who has been trying to get accepted by a med school in Belgium.

8). Former roommate says she'll pay utilities "when she can." Three months later, still not a red cent.

9). You call roommate's mother to complain about irresponsibility. Mother responds by calling phone company, cutting off your phone service while you're at work.

10). You open new phone account in old roommate's name, run up enormous bill the first month with no intention of paying. Give irate phone company your roommate's new address.

HOW CAN I MISS YOU WHEN YOU WON'T STAY AWAY?: The Ex-Roommate as Guest

Your relationship was cordial, but you weren't the best of friends. Now your roommate has decided that the grass is greener in another city, but still wants to stay in touch with folks in your town through frequent visits.

But does your ex-roommate ever stay with the friends or business contacts she is really returning to see? Of course not. She stays with you. You, like Mom, may not be the most exciting person in her life, but you're dependable, and she knows what you're likely to have in your refrigerator.

Hosting a former roommate is unlike hosting any other guest. There is a weird sense of *déjà vu*. In some ways it's just like the old days. She certainly makes herself at home more easily than your average guest. On the one hand, it seems only natural. On the other, it bothers you. She doesn't really live there anymore, does she?

Who else would think of giving less than 48 hours' notice for a week-long visit?

You can't put her off by saying you'll be: 1). out of town; or, 2). very busy. She'll just: 1). use the set of keys she's kept "just in case"; and, 2). won't be any trouble at all.

You barely see your ex during the visit, but evidence of her presence is everywhere. Luggage is strewn about, damp shirts hang in the bathroom, strange drugs occupy the medicine chest, and the phone rings constantly for her.

Since she left, your roommate has become a free-lance interior-decorating consultant. The same person who never bothered to put a poster up on the wall, much less lift a paintbrush, is now intensely concerned that you've painted the living room yellow.

You almost forgot the little things about her that used to bother you, but within hours—in some cases, minutes—your resentment level is even higher than when she used to live with you.

There are invariably at least a few of her possessions left at your place. She removes them one by one, in order from most useful to least useful.

The things she doesn't take with her, she asks you to ship, promising to reimburse you right away. The second time you ship C.O.D. Then she asks you to cart her possessions over to obscure acquaintances who live in remote neighborhoods of your city. This is because they will soon be traveling to her city to take advantage of the hospitality you will never enjoy.

Your ex still finds your city endlessly fascinating and visits frequently. You suspect this is cheap nostalgia as much as anything. But you really can't pay your ex back in kind, because you have absolutely no desire to visit her city. Even if you did, you suspect you wouldn't get treated as well as you treat her. After all, you couldn't possibly presume to treat her new place like your second home, could you?

LOST IN THE PURGE

It's the morning after your roommate has finally moved out. You both handled it with a certain style and graciousness. But let's face it, you wanted her gone and she wanted to be going.

You get up a list of numbers of potential roommates and sit down to breakfast. You decide an omelette would be nice, but the omelette pan doesn't seem to be in its usual spot. You drag all the copper out of the cabinets—no pan. It is then that the reality bonks you over the head.

She took it.

How *dare* she take it?

She *knew* it was yours.

My *God,* she took it!

You calm down. When it comes time to divide up the last phone bill, you will call her. You will inquire politely if in packing she hadn't mistakenly taken your omelette pan. Would she kindly return it, if it wouldn't be too much trouble?

You walk into the bathroom to take a shower. You turn on the faucet. The shower head goes flying into the tub and water gushes from the bare tap like Victoria Falls. You rip back the shower curtain. Wait a minute.

Where is the shower curtain? That was the shower curtain your mother sent when you told her the nice pink and blue one got all moldy.

You turn off the water and stalk to the closet to get the tool kit Dad gave you for college graduation. Dear Lord, *this is unbelievable!*

She took the *tool kit!*

Your rage has now reached uncontrollable proportions. You fly about the apartment, throwing things, knocking things over. Finally, you collapse on the couch.

You decide not to wait for the phone bill to come. You're going to call her up right now. If she doesn't return the *stolen* items immediately, you're going to call the police.

Yes, the *police!*

You are feeling completely absurd, taken and other terrible things.

You stagger to your bookshelf to get the book that is always your comfort in times of stress, the one you read over and over when Mr. Kitty died: *Notes to Myself* by Hugh Prather. *Aghhhhhhhhhh!*

When you regain consciousness, you try to recall whether any of your friends own firearms. Of course, they don't.

In your stupor, you stagger back to the bathroom, take three aspirins, get dressed, and go out. You buy a shower curtain, a wrench and a copy of *Notes to Myself*. You return, make scrambled eggs, and call in to your office sick. Three hours late.

Then your eye fixes on an object in the corner of the room. *Teddy.* The one possession you can't believe she would have left. You shake hands with Teddy. You pick Teddy up and walk into the kitchen with him. You take the electric carving knife out of the drawer and *filet* Teddy.

Just as the stuffing begins to settle, the doorbell rings. As you stand holding the disemboweled Teddy in your arms, your horror-struck former roommate, holding two bags full of the missing possessions, gasps, "Gary helped me pack and took these by mistake!"

Now
that you've read this book,
you know
what you're up
against.

Use to Mark the
Page That Tells
Your Roommates
What They Need
to Hear

Roommate
Conflict
Avoidance
Card

Are your roommates in this book? Should they be in a book? Send us your tales of roommate woe, horror and glory. We may be able to include them in a sequel to *What Color Is Your Toothbrush?* All letters become the property of Kate Kelly, Richard Davis and Jeff Stone. Please address your stories to:

ROOMMATES
c/o East Chelsea Press
43 West 16th Street, Suite 5D
New York, N.Y. 10011